Bones and Muscles

Angela Royston

W
FRANKLIN WATTS
LONDON • SYDNEY

First published in 2007 by Franklin Watts

Copyright © Franklin Watts 2007

Franklin Watts
338 Euston Road
London NW1 3BH

Franklin Watts Australia
Level 17/207 Kent Street
Sydney, NSW 2000

Series editor: Sarah Peutrill
Art director: Jonathan Hair
Design: Mo Choy
Consultant: Peter Riley
Photographer: Paul Bricknell
Illustrations: Ian Thompson

Picture credits: Peter Adams/zefa/Corbis: 17. H. Benser/zefa/Corbis: 28b. Dept. of Clinical Radiology, Salisbury District Hospital/SPL: 28t. Laureen Morgane/zefa/Corbis: 24. David Raymer/Corbis: 20. Paul A. Souders/Corbis: 15. Hattie Young/SPL: 29t.

A CIP catalogue record for this book is available from the British Library.

Dewey number: 612.7
ISBN: 978 0 7496 7633 9

Printed in China

Franklin Watts is a division of Hachette Children's Books, an Hachette Livre UK company.

Contents

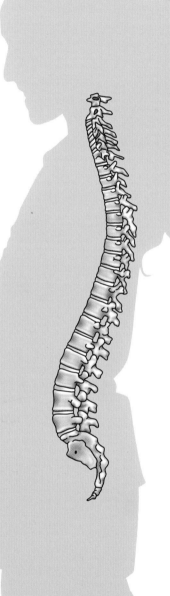

Under your skin

You can move different parts of your body – your arms, legs, head and back. You can also move your whole body from one place to another. How do you do this? The answer lies under your skin!

Moving part of your body

Under your skin are fat, soft muscles and hard bones. The fat and muscles make a soft padding between your skin and some of your bones. Muscles make your bones move.

▲
You have two long bones in your lower arm and one long bone in your upper arm. Muscles move these bones to move your arm – to make it bend, straighten and twist.

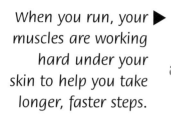

When you run, your ▶ *muscles are working hard under your skin to help you take longer, faster steps.*

Moving your whole body

You move your feet and legs to get from place to place. Muscles work together to bend your knees and move the bones in your legs and feet.

Your muscles wrap ▼ *around your bones.*

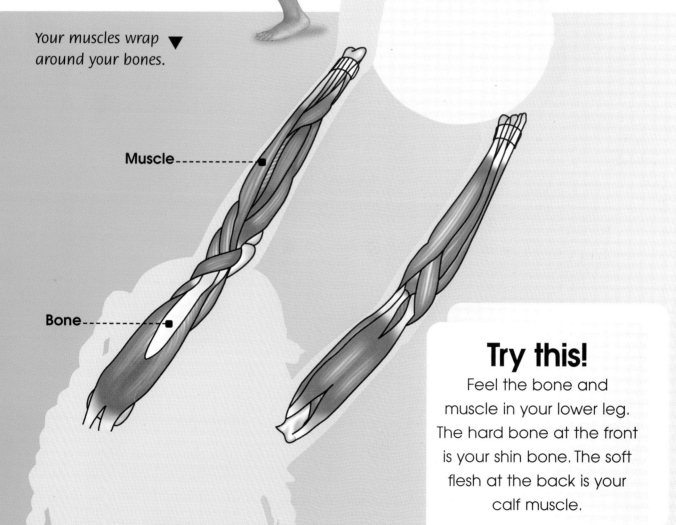

Muscle- - - - - - - - - - - -■

Bone- - - - - - - - - -■

Try this!

Feel the bone and muscle in your lower leg. The hard bone at the front is your shin bone. The soft flesh at the back is your calf muscle.

Your skeleton

Your skeleton is made up of all the bones in your body. Your skeleton is a framework inside your body that gives you your shape. Without bones, you would flop like a jelly.

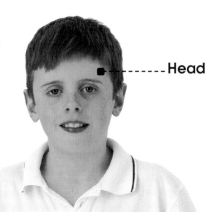

Head

Arm

Each bone has its ▶ own name. This is different from the name you give the outside part of the body. For example, the bone inside your head is called the skull.

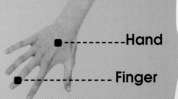

Hand

Finger

Bony framework

When you were born, you had more than 350 different bones. As you grow up, some bones join together to make one bone. Adults have just 208 bones.

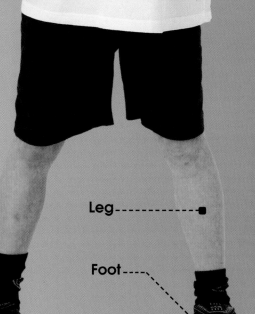

Leg

Foot

Strong and rigid

Bones are hard and very strong. They do not break easily and they do not bend. You can't bend your lower arm because the bones inside are rigid.

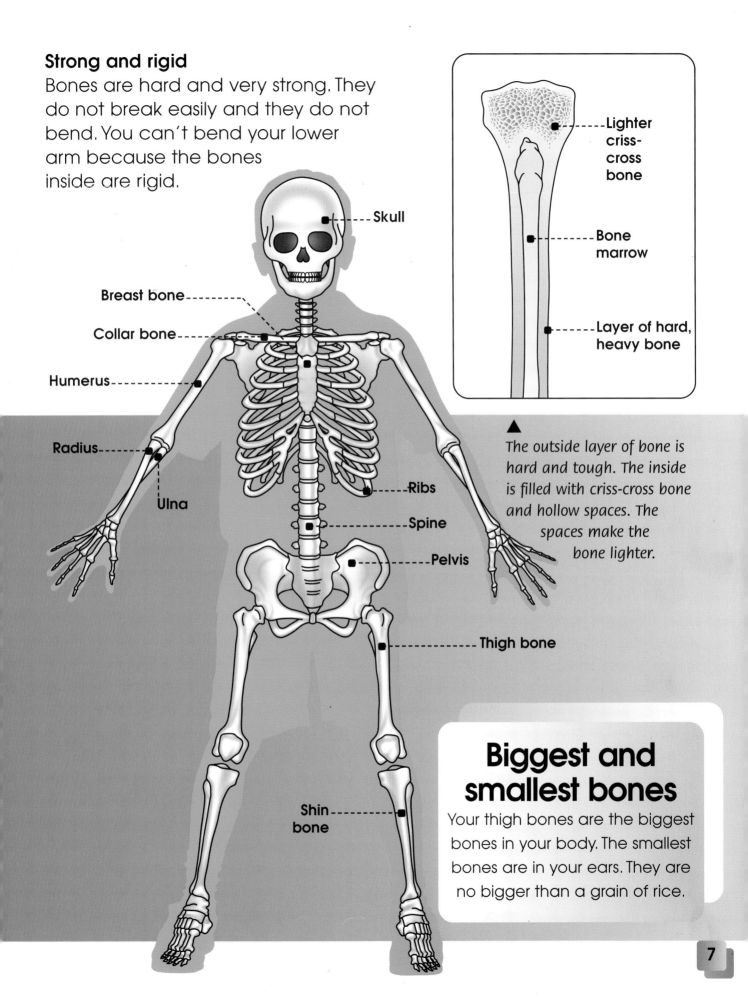

Skull

Breast bone

Collar bone

Humerus

Radius

Ulna

Ribs

Spine

Pelvis

Thigh bone

Shin bone

Lighter criss-cross bone

Bone marrow

Layer of hard, heavy bone

▲

The outside layer of bone is hard and tough. The inside is filled with criss-cross bone and hollow spaces. The spaces make the bone lighter.

Biggest and smallest bones

Your thigh bones are the biggest bones in your body. The smallest bones are in your ears. They are no bigger than a grain of rice.

Body armour

Some bones protect important parts of your body called organs. These bones are like a suit of armour around your brain, heart and lungs.

Bony helmet
If you gently tap your head, you can feel your skull under the skin. This bone surrounds your brain – the organ that controls almost every part of your body.

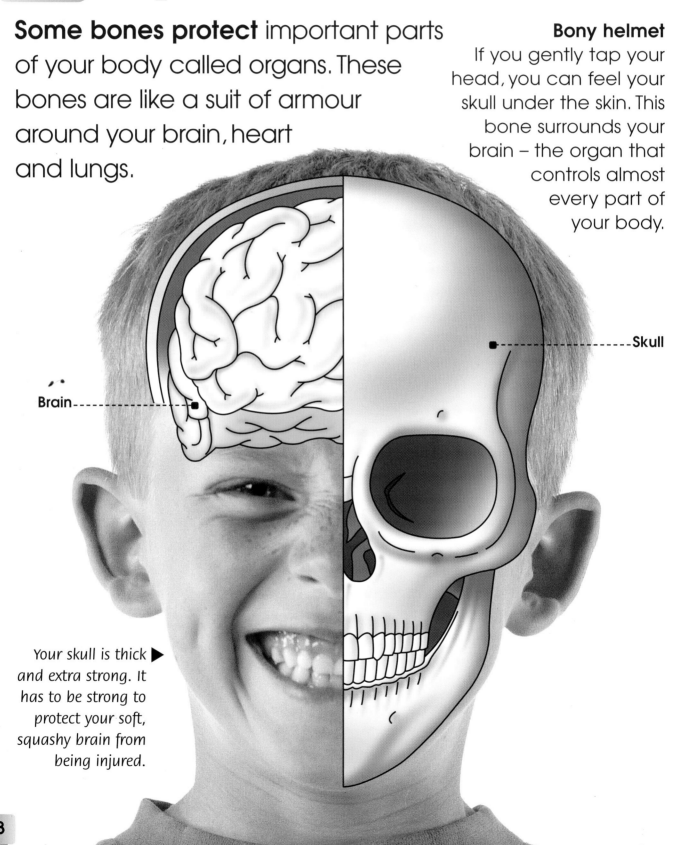

Brain

Skull

◀ Your skull is thick and extra strong. It has to be strong to protect your soft, squashy brain from being injured.

Rib cage

Your ribs are curved, narrow bones. They protect two important organs – your heart and lungs. Your lungs take in air when you breathe in and your heart pumps blood around your body.

Under your chest your ribs curve around from your spine to your breast bone. They form a rigid cage over your heart and lungs. ▼

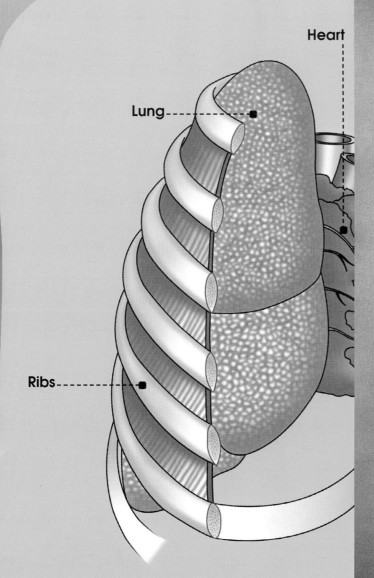

Heart

Lung

Ribs

Try this!

Try to count how many ribs you have on each side of your body. You can feel your ribs on the side of your body, under your arms.

Joints

A joint is where two or more bones meet. Joints hold the ends of the bones together and allow them to move easily.

Moving bones

You can only move your bones at your joints. You move your arms at your shoulders and elbows. You move your legs at your hips and knees.

Different joints allow you to ▶ move in different ways. Your shoulders let you move your arm in all directions, but at the knee you can only swing your leg backwards and forwards.

Try this!

Try moving different joints in your body. How many ways does each one move?

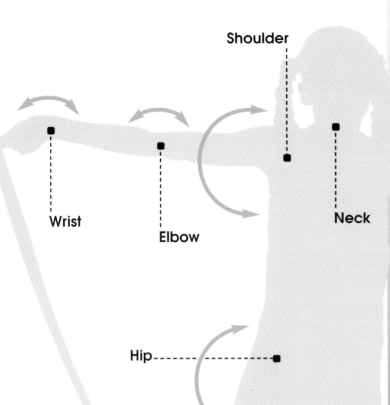

Shoulder

Wrist

Elbow

Neck

Hip

Knee

Ankle

Joints have different names.
These are the main joints.

Ligaments are like straps. ▶
They hold the ends of the
bone together in the joint.

Inside a joint

The ends of the bones are covered with soft cartilage. The cartilage stops the bones rubbing together. Some joints, such as your knee, also contain liquid to help them move smoothly.

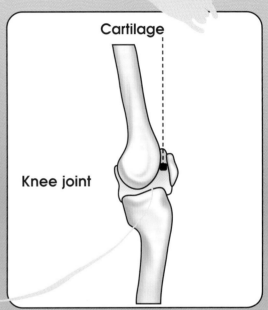

Cartilage

Knee joint

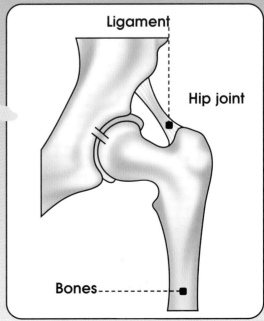

Ligament

Hip joint

Bones

Fingers and thumbs

You use your hands to pick up and hold things such as pens, forks and books. The joints in your fingers and thumbs allow you to do this.

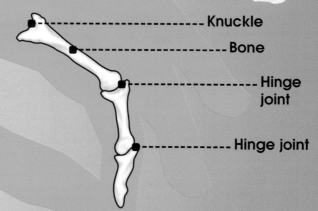

Bending your fingers

The joints inside your fingers are hinge joints. They only let your fingers bend and straighten. They work like the hinges that join a door to the wall and let it open and close.

Knuckle ---------------------

Bone ---------------------

Hinge joint ---------------------

Hinge joint ---------------------

◄

Each finger has two hinge joints that divide the finger into three parts. You move the whole finger using the joint inside your knuckle.

12

Moving your thumb

As well as bending and straightening your thumb, you can move it around in circles. This is because it is joined to your hand by a saddle joint. This allows a wide range of movements.

Try this!

Touch each finger of your hand with your thumb. Only humans, apes and most monkeys can do this! This is because we have opposable thumbs. This special ability allows us to write and use other tools.

Saddle joint

You use your thumb and fingers to hold a pen or a paintbrush. You make many small but exact movements when you write.

▼

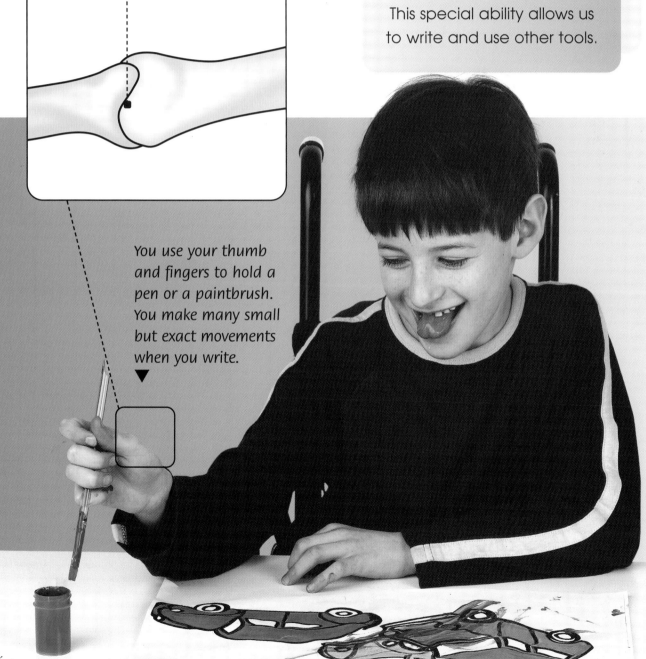

13

Shoulders and hips

The joints inside your shoulders and hips give more movement than any other joint. They are called ball and socket joints.

The top of the thigh bone is shaped like a ball. It fits into a round space, called the socket, inside the hip.

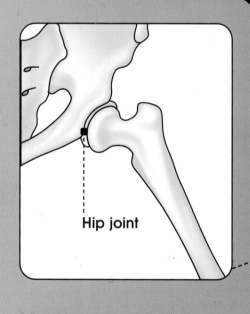

Hip joint

Moving your hips
Your leg moves from your hip. As you swing it forwards or out in a circle, the top of the thigh bone moves around inside the hip joint.

Swinging your arms

You can reach out in almost every direction with your arms. But the joint inside your shoulder stops you swinging your arms as far backwards as you can forwards.

Ligaments around each shoulder joint keep the top of your arm bone inside your shoulder joint. They stop your arm from slipping out.

▼

Doing the splits

Some people can move their legs so far apart they can do the splits! This is because their hip joints can move further than other people's.

Your neck

The joint inside your neck allows you to nod your head and turn it from side to side. You can even see behind you just by twisting your head!

Moving your head

The joint inside your neck is a pivot joint. A round hole at the bottom of the skull fits over a spike at the top of the spine.

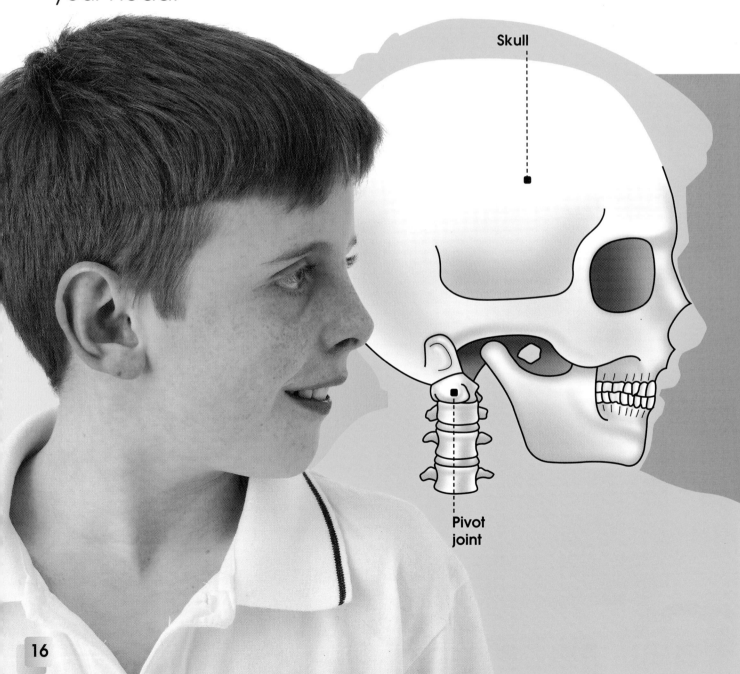

Skull

Pivot joint

16

Holding up your head

Your neck not only lets you move your head, it also holds it in place. The spike inside the joint stops your head slipping off your neck.

This girl's neck is so strong she can carry a heavy weight on her head. She balances it so that her skull is not tilted on her neck joint.
▼

◀ As you turn your head, your skull turns around the spike inside your neck joint. The bone around the pivot supports the skull and allows it to rock up and down so you can nod your head.

Try this!
Balance a book on your head. Make sure your head is perfectly straight. How far can you walk with it?

Your spine

Your spine is an amazing column of knobbly bones that hold your body together. Your arms, legs, head and all the bones in your trunk are attached to your spine.

Back bones

The knobbly bones in your spine are called vertebrae. They fit into each other to make a strong column of bones.

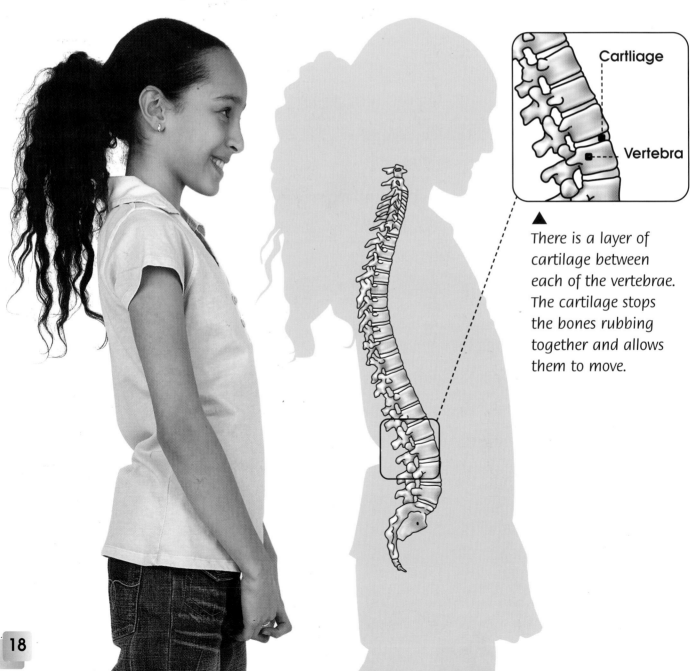

Cartliage

Vertebra

▲
There is a layer of cartilage between each of the vertebrae. The cartilage stops the bones rubbing together and allows them to move.

Bending and twisting

The vertebrae and cartilage allow you to bend and twist to one side or the other. If your spine had just one bone, you could not bend at all.

When you bend, the vertebrae ▶ inside your waist move a little, but they still stay fitted together.

Try this!

Move your fingers up and down your spine. Can you feel the knobbly vertebrae? Feel the vertebrae at your waist move as you bend over and straighten up.

Muscles move your bones

Most of your bones are covered by muscles. You have about 650 different muscles, which gives your body a soft, rounded shape. Muscles work by pulling your bones to move them.

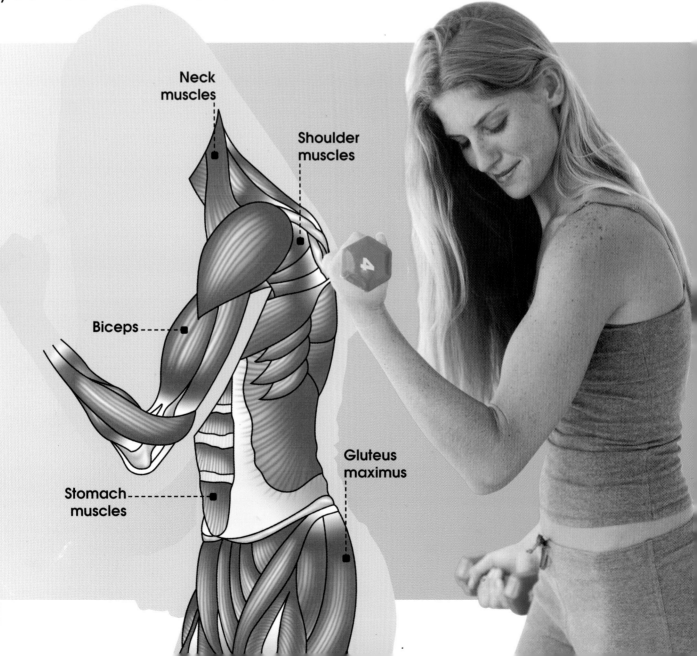

Neck muscles

Shoulder muscles

Biceps

Stomach muscles

Gluteus maximus

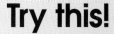

Try this!

Hold your calf and point your toes. Can you feel your calf muscle get tighter and harder?

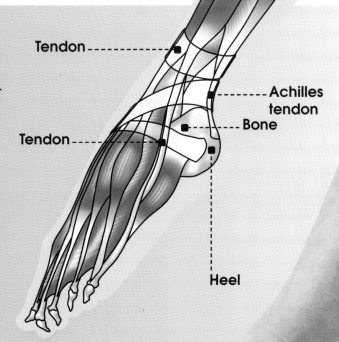

Calf
muscle

Tendon ------------

Achilles
tendon

Tendon ------------

Bone

Heel

Mapping the muscles

Muscles pull your bones, but not the bones they cover. For example, your thigh muscle moves your lower leg.

How a muscle works

The muscles that move your foot are in your calf. They are attached to the bones in your foot by strong cords called tendons.

When your calf muscles ▶ contract, the tendons pull your foot so it moves at the ankle joint. The main tendon is the Achilles tendon.

Moving your elbow

When a muscle contracts it pulls a bone. Muscles only pull – they cannot push. This means that most muscles work in teams to pull a bone in different directions.

Bending your arm
The muscles that bend and straighten your lower arm are in your upper arm. The muscle that bends your arm is called the biceps.

Ulna

Biceps

Tendon

Elbow joint

▲

The tendon from the biceps is attached to the ulna, one of the bones inside the lower arm. When the biceps contracts, the tendon pulls up the lower arm.

Straightening your arm

A different muscle straightens your arm. It is called the triceps and it is at the back of your upper arm. When the triceps contracts, the biceps relaxes.

Try this!

Hold your upper arm while you bend and straighten your arm. Can you feel the biceps and triceps muscles contracting and relaxing?

The tendon from the triceps passes over your elbow and is also attached to the ulna in your lower arm.

▼

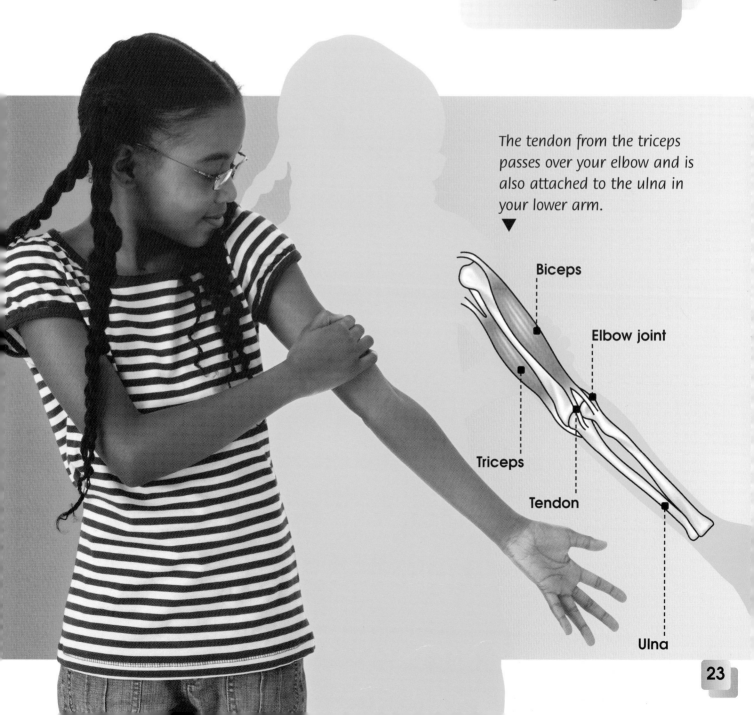

Biceps

Elbow joint

Triceps

Tendon

Ulna

Exercise

Exercise makes your muscles and joints become stronger. Most exercise uses many muscles working together. You are not usually aware which muscles you are using – you contract and relax them without thinking.

Swimming
Swimming exercises nearly all your muscles. The more you exercise, the better your muscles work and the longer you can keep going before you get tired.

You move your arms, legs and head when you swim. This uses muscles in your stomach, chest, neck and back as well ◀ as in your arms and legs.

Dancing

Dancing helps you to balance and exercises muscles in your stomach, arms and legs. Dancing exercises your joints as well as your muscles.

Dancing helps your muscles ▶ and joints work better.

Biggest muscles

The biggest muscles are the gluteus maximi in your bottom. You use them to stand up and to run. They also give you a soft cushion to sit on.

Moving your face

Not all your muscles move bones. The muscles in your face move your lips, cheeks and brow. A tiny muscle opens your eyelids. You use it every time you blink!

Eating and talking
The lower jaw is the only bone in your head that you can move. You move it to open and shut your mouth when you eat and when you talk.

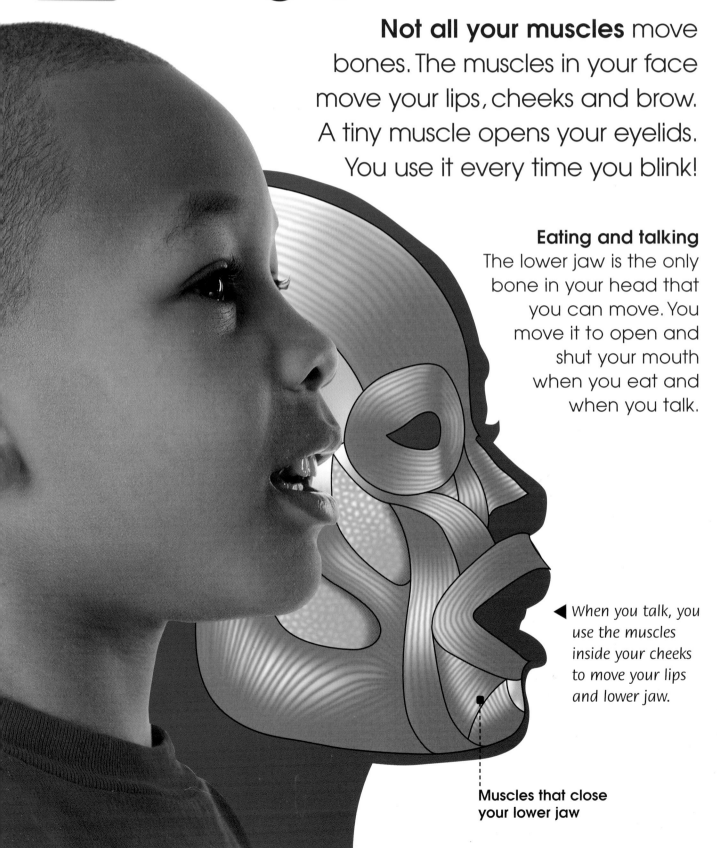

◄ *When you talk, you use the muscles inside your cheeks to move your lips and lower jaw.*

Muscles that close your lower jaw

Smiling and frowning

When you feel happy or sad, puzzled, angry or bored, the expression on your face changes. Muscles in your face work together to make different expressions.

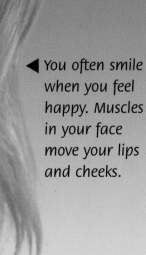

Strongest muscle

The strongest muscle in your body is the one that closes your mouth. You use it when you eat.

◀ You often smile when you feel happy. Muscles in your face move your lips and cheeks.

Breaks and sprains

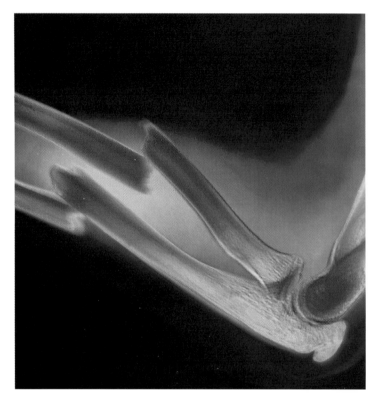

You may injure a bone or joint if you have a bad fall. You may break a bone, or you may sprain a joint. Breaks and sprains can take several weeks to heal.

◀ *The X-ray shows broken bones in an arm. A doctor straightens the broken bones and wraps a special bandage around the arm. New bone grows across the breaks to make the arm whole again.*

Broken bone
A broken arm or leg is very painful. A doctor wraps a special bandage around the broken bone and joint. The bandage makes a hard cast that protects the bone while it heals.

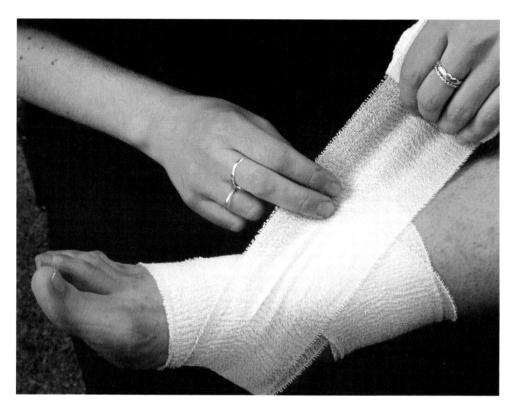

Sprained ankle

A sprain is when you tear a ligament around a joint. If you sprain your ankle, for example, the joint will swell up and be very painful.

◀ A nurse wraps a stretchy bandage around the sprain. The bandage supports the ankle until it heals.

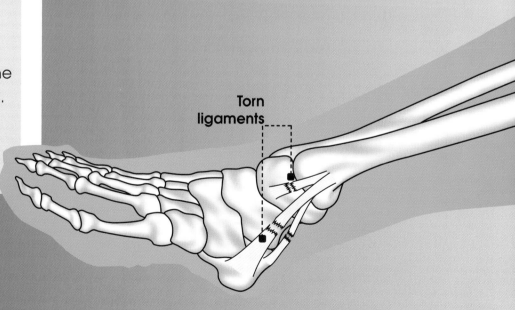

Ice pack

If you sprain a joint, hold an ice pack on the joint for a few minutes. The ice pack will reduce the swelling.

Torn ligaments

Glossary

bone marrow
A fatty substance inside long bones.

bones
The hard parts of the body that lie under your skin and muscle.

brain
The organ that controls most of the things that happen in your body, including your thoughts and feelings.

cartilage
The soft, squashy material that is found at the ends of bones and in the flap of your ear.

cast
A hard shell in the shape of an arm or leg or other injured part of the body.

expression
The look on your face that shows what you are feeling or thinking.

gluteus maximus (plural glutei maximi)
The large muscle in the buttock.

heart
An organ made of a special kind of muscle. The heart pumps blood through your arteries to all parts of your body.

joint
The place where two or more bones meet and fit together.

knuckle
The joint in your hand where one end of your finger meets your hand. You can see your knuckles on the back of your hand.

ligament
The strap that holds the bones in a joint together.

lungs
The organs that take in air when you breathe in.

muscle
A fleshy tissue that is able to contract and relax to move a part of the body.

opposable thumb
A thumb which can touch each of the fingers on the same hand.

organ
A part of the body, such as the brain, heart, stomach and lungs, that does a particular job.

rigid
Something is rigid when it is stiff and unbending.

tendon
The strong cord that joins a muscle to the bone it moves.

vertebra
One of the bones in your spine.

X-ray
A special kind of photograph that shows the bones inside your body.

Further information
WEBSITES
www.bbc.co.uk/science/ humanbody/body
This site gives you games and interactive information about the human body.

www.kidshealth.org
This site gives you information about your body. Click on the section called 'for kids'.

Index

These are the lists of contents for each title in *Your Body - Inside and Out*

Bones and Muscles

Under your skin • Your skeleton • Body armour • Joints • Fingers and thumbs • Shoulders and hips • Your neck • Your spine • Muscles move your bones • Moving your elbow • Exercise • Moving your face • Breaks and sprains

Food and Digestion

Food is fuel • Energy foods: starches • Energy foods: sugars • Body-building foods • Fats and oils • Fruit and vegetables • What happens to food? • Chew and swallow • Into the intestines • Absorbing food • Water and waste • Problems with foods • A healthy diet

Growing

The cycle of life • Producing babies • Inside the womb • Everyone is different • A newborn baby • From six months to one year old • Toddlers • From toddler to child • Young children • From child to adult • Fully grown • Getting older • Keeping healthy

Heart and Lungs

The heart and lungs • The heart is a muscle • The heart is a pump • What is blood for? • We need oxygen • Your ribs move • Lungs are sponges • Gases in and out • The blood system • The four-part heart • A healthy heart • Strong heart and lungs • Checking your pulse

Senses

What are the senses? • Your brain • Seeing • Inside the eye • Wearing glasses • Hearing • Inside your eye • Hard of hearing • Smelling • Tasting • Touching • Heat and pain • Working together

Teeth and Hair

Looking good • What are teeth made of? • Shapes of teeth • Two sets of teeth • Cleaning teeth • Stronger and straighter • Tooth decay • What causes tooth decay? • How hair grows • Protecting your skin • Looking after hair • Head lice • Treating head lice